CHRISTMAS EN

Contemporary Arrangements of Christmas Favorites

BOOK 2

arranged by
Melody Bober

MW00824172

CONTENTS

What Child Is This?

Traditional English

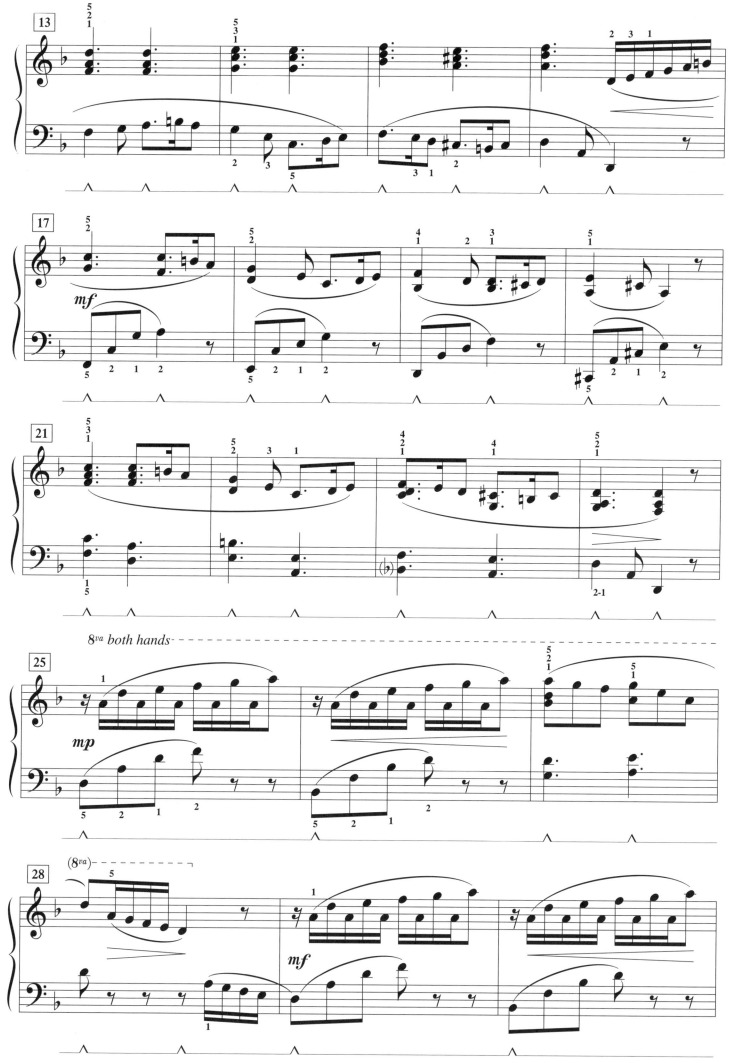

4

Deck the Hall

Traditional Welsh

FJH1239

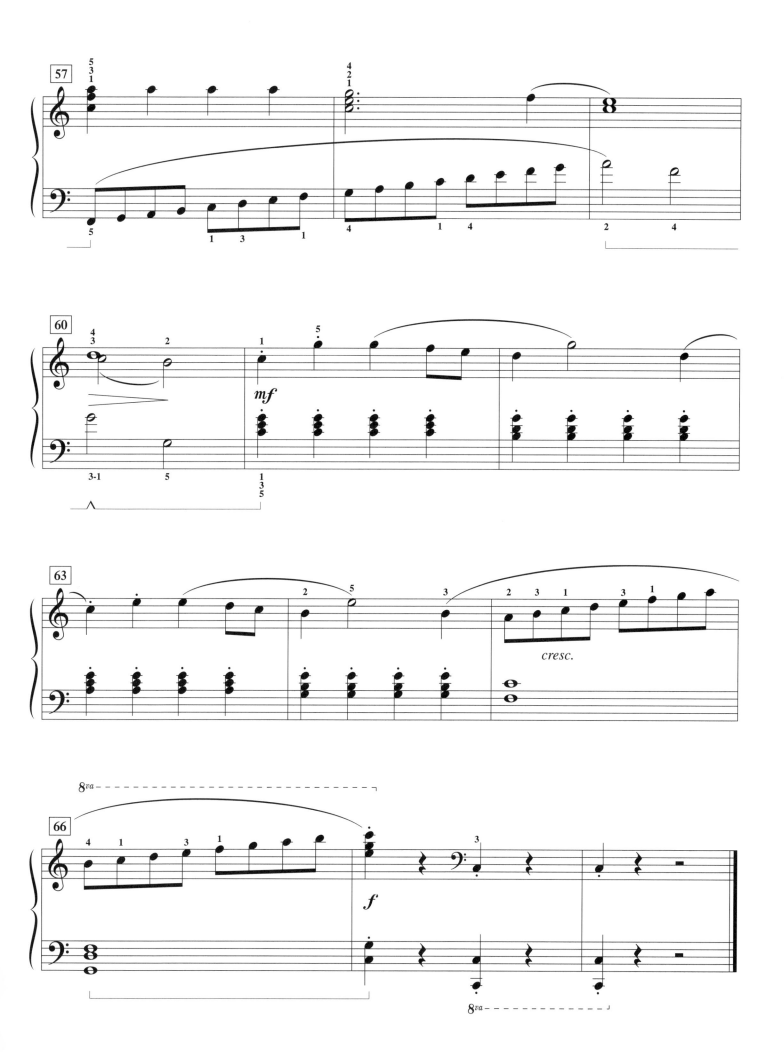

Away in a Manger

**Music by
James R. Murray**

12

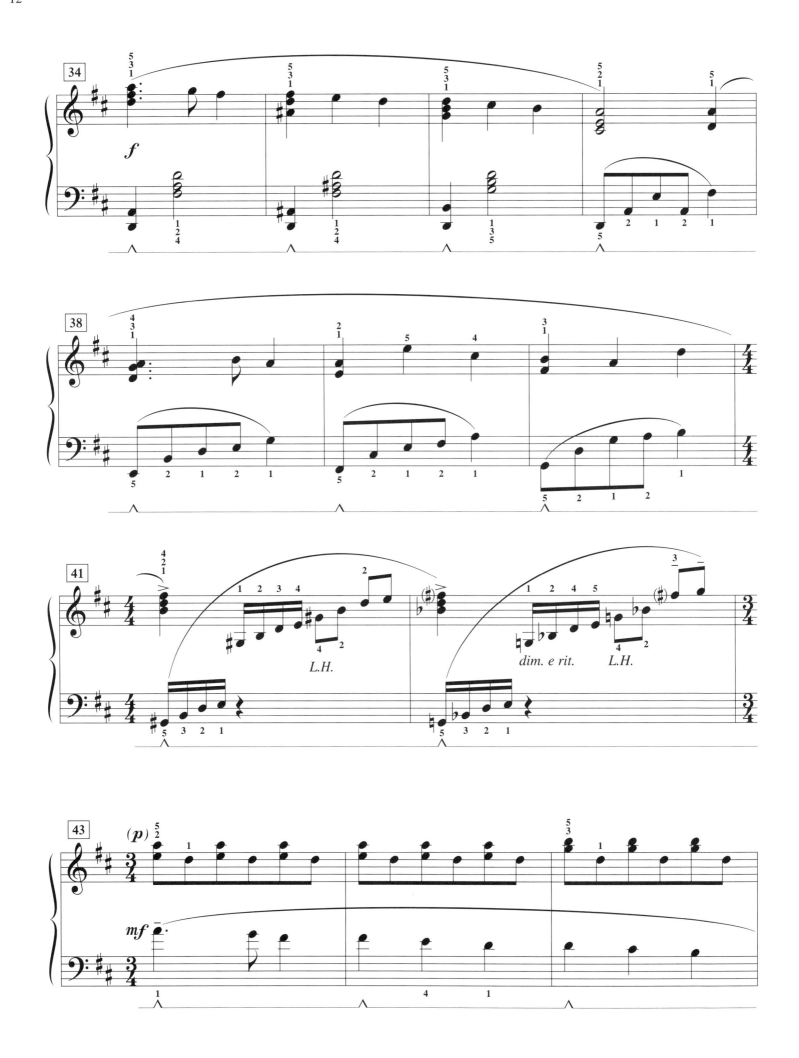

He Is Born, the Holy Child

Traditional French

Good Christian Men, Rejoice

Traditional German

Silent Night

Words by
Joseph Mohr
(adapted)

Music by
Franz Grüber

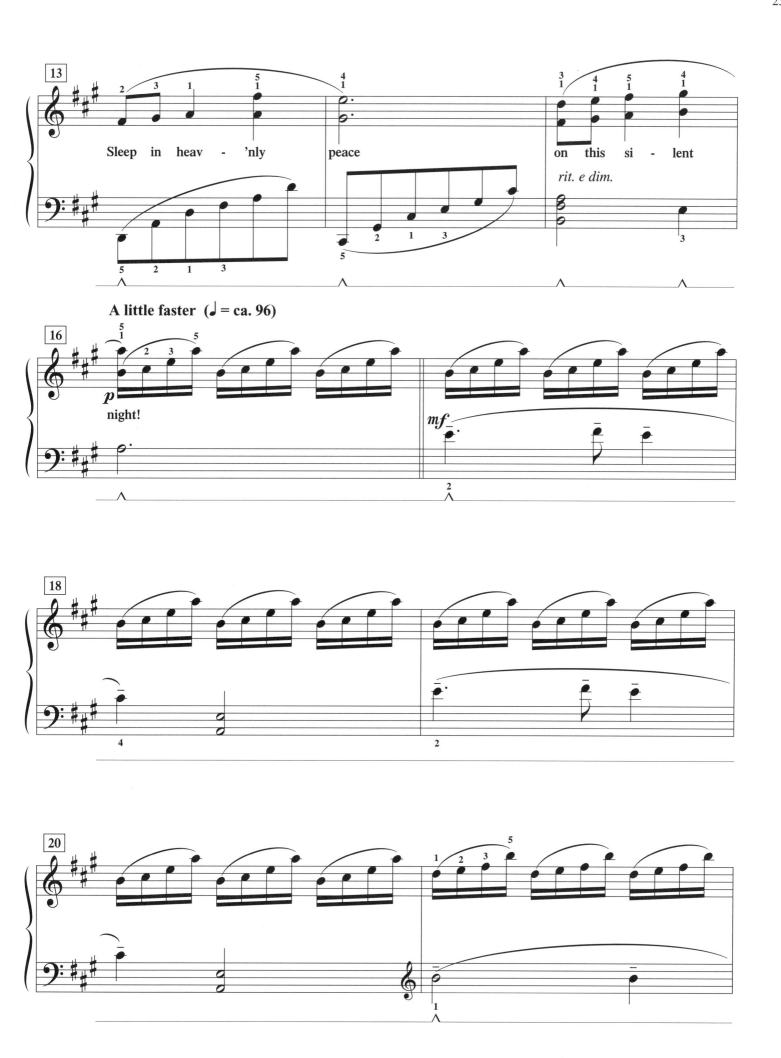

God Rest Ye Merry, Gentlemen

Traditional English